The Batt   of Cintla

Daniel G. Brinton

Alpha Editions

This edition published in 2021

ISBN : 9789354593062

Design and Setting By
Alpha Editions
www.alphaedis.com
Email - info@alphaedis.com

THE BATTLE AND THE RUINS OF CINTLA.

By Daniel G. Brinton, M. D.

The first battle on the American continent in which horses were used was that of Cintla in Tabasco, March, 1519, the European troops being under the leadership of Hernando Cortes.

This fact attaches something more than an ordinary historic interest to the engagement, at least enough to make it desirable to ascertain its precise locality and its proper name. Both of these are in doubt, as well as the ethnic stock to which the native tribe belonged which opposed the Spanish soldiery on the occasion. I propose to submit these questions to a re-examination, and also to describe from unpublished material the ruins which,—as I believe—, mark the spot of this first important encounter of the two races on American soil.

The engagement itself has been described by all the historians of Cortes' famous conquest of Mexico, as it was the first brilliant incident of that adventure. We have at least four accounts of it from participants. One prepared under the eye of Cortes himself, one by the anonymous historian of his expedition, a third by Cortes' companion-in-arms, the redoubtable Bernal Diaz del Castillo, and a fourth by Andres de Tapia.3-1

The most satisfactory narrative, however, is given by the chaplain of Cortes, Francisco de Gomara, and I shall briefly rehearse his story, adding a few points from other contemporary writers.3-2

Cortes with his armada cast anchor at the mouth of the River Grijalva in March, 1519. The current being strong and the bar shallow, he with about eighty men proceeded in boats up the river for about two miles, when they descried on the bank a large Indian village. It was surrounded with a wooden palisade, having turrets and loopholes from which to hurl stones and darts. The houses within were built of tiles laid in mortar, or of sun-dried brick (adobes), and were roofed with straw or split trees. The chief temple had spacious rooms, and its dependences surrounded a court yard.

The interpreter Aguilar, a Spaniard who had lived with the Mayas in Yucatan, could readily speak the tongue of the village, which was therefore a Mayan dialect. The natives told him that the town was named Potonchan, which Aguilar translated "the place that smells or stinks," an etymology probably correct in a general way.

The natives were distrustful, and opposed the landing of the Europeans rather with words and gestures than with blows. Their warriors approached Cortes in large boats, called in their tongue *tahucup*, and refused him permission to land.

After some parleying, Cortes withdrew to an island in the river near by, and as night drew on, he sent to the ships for reinforcements, and despatched some of the troops to look for a ford from the island to the mainland; which they easily found.

The next morning he landed some of his men by the boats, and attacked the village on the water side, while another detachment crossed the ford and making a circuit assaulted it in the rear. The Indians were prepared, having sent their women and children away. They were in number about four hundred, and made at first a brisk resistance, but being surprised by the rear assault, soon fled in dismay. No Spaniard was killed, though many were wounded.

Cortes established himself in the village and landed most of his troops and ten out of his thirteen horses. When his men were rested and the injured had had their wounds dressed with fat taken from dead Indians4-1 (!) he sent out three detachments on foot to reconnoitre.

After marching a distance which is not stated, but which could not have been many miles, they came to an extensive plain covered with maize fields, temples and houses. This was Cintla. There were many warriors gathered there, and after a sharp skirmish the Spaniards fell back.

Having thus learned the ground, Cortes prepared for a decisive battle, as also did the natives. The latter gathered at Cintla in five divisions of eight thousand men each, as the chroniclers aver.

Cortes had about five hundred men including some Cuban Indians. The main detachment proceeded on foot by the high road, the cavalry along a path in the woods, and another detachment by a third route. The country was swampy and cut with canals, offering serious obstacles to the horses. It was not until the infantry had been for some time closely engaged with the enemy on the plain of Cintla, and rather severely handled, that the cavalry reached the spot. Their appearance, together with the noise and fatal effect of the musketry, soon struck terror to the hearts of the natives—their ranks broke and they fled. Gomara estimates that there were about three hundred of them killed, which is likely enough; while Bishop De las Casas puts the slain at thirty thousand!5-1

Such was the battle of Cintla. It broke the spirits of the natives, and soon their chieftain, named Tabasco, from whom the river and the province were later called, came in, and offered his submission. Cortes took possession of the land in the name of the King of Spain, and erected a large cross in the chief temple of Potonchan. He remained there several days longer before proceeding on his voyage.

The Name Cintla.—Of the contemporary authorities, only two give the name of the place at or near which the battle was fought.

One of these is Bernal Diaz, who writes it twice, spelling it both times *Cintia.*[5-2] The other is Gomara, who gives *Cintla*, the form which I believe to be correct. Through following some less reliable authorities a number of writers, among them Prescott and his editor Mr. J. F. Kirk, Orozco y Berra, etc., and their copyists, have deformed this word into *Ceutla*.

The most obvious derivation of Cintla is from the Nahuatl language, in which *Cintla* means a dried ear of maize; *Cintlan*, a place where dried ears are, a cornfield. Most of the places in Tabasco became known to the Spaniards under their Nahuatl appellatives through interpreters in that tongue, and because most of the territory had been subjected to the powerful sway of the Montezumas.

Still, Cintla may also be a Mayan word. It may be a nominal form from the verb *tzen-tah*, and would then have the signification, "a built-up place," or one well stocked with provisions; or, it may be a patronymic from the Tzentals, the tribe which occupied this region at the time, as I shall proceed to show.

The Native Tribe.—There is no question but that the native tribe which took part in this combat belonged to the Mayan stock. All the accounts agree that Aguilar, the Spaniard whom Cortes found in Yucatan as a captive, and who had learned to speak the Mayan tongue, communicated with the natives without difficulty. This is conclusive as to their ethnic position.

Further evidence, if needed, is offered by the native names and words preserved in the accounts. The term for their large canoes, *tahucup*, is from the Maya *tahal*, to swim, and *kop*, that which is hollow, or hollowed out. The name *potonchan*, Aguilar translated as, "the place that stinks" (lugar que hiede). He evidently understood it as derived from the Maya verb *tunhal*, to stink, with the intensive prefix *pot* (which is not unusual in the tongue, as *pot-hokan*, very evident, etc.). The historian Herrera, on some authority not known to me, further explains this term as one of contempt applied to the people there, meaning rude and barbarous;6-1 as we should say, using the same metaphor, "stinkards."

Tabasco is said by Bernal Diaz to have been the name of the principal chief of the eight provinces or tribes, who together opposed the Spaniards. For this reason I would reject the derivation from the Nahuatl, proposed by Rovirosa,—*tlalli*, earth, *paltic*, wet or swampy, *co*, in,6-2—however appropriate it would be geographically; and also that from the Maya, *tazcoob*, "deceived," referring to the deceptions practiced on the Spaniards,—which is defended by Orozco y Berra6-3; and I should accept that which I find suggested by Dr. Berendt in his manuscript work on Mayan geographical names. He reads *Tabasco* as a slightly corrupt form of the Maya *T'ah-uaxac-coh*, "our (or the) master of the eight lions," referring to the eight districts or gentes of the tribe. This is significant and appropriate, the jaguar, the American lion, being a very common emblem in the ruins of Cintla.

The branch of the Mayan stock which occupied the litoral of the province of Tabasco at that time were those later known as the Tzentals (otherwise spelled Zendal or Tzeltal). By some writers they have been called the Chontals of Tobasco, *chontal*, as is well known, being merely a common noun in Nahuatl to express foreigners or barbarians. Their identity with the modern Tzentals of Chiápas has been established by the researches of Dr. Berendt.

The Tzental is a dialect closely akin to pure Maya, though it was believed by Dr. Berendt to present nearer relations than the Maya proper to the dialect of the Huastecas, a segregated idiom of the Mayan family, spoken near Tampico.

The Locality.—Until M. Désiré Charnay brought out the results of the Lorillard expedition in his handsome work, "The Ancient Cities of the New World,"[6-4] no one, so far as I know, had expressed any doubt that Cintla was situated near the mouth of the great river, the Rio de Tabasco, formed by the confluence of the Usumacinta and the Rio de Grijalva, and emptying into the bay of Campeche, 18° 35', north latitude.

M. Charnay did not visit the ruins of Cintla nor the site of Potonchan, which I am about to describe; but he did make an examination of the ruins of Comalcalco, about thirty miles west of Cintla; and as they are of notable magnitude, he proceeds to argue that they represent the ancient Cintla, of the victory of Cortes.

The arguments on which he founds this contention may be briefly stated. They are that the accounts refer to two entrances to the river (*dos bocas*) while the Tabasco has but one; that the bar of Tabasco now admits vessels of 300 tons, whereas Cortes speaks of it as too shallow for his caravels; that Herrera says Cortes retired to a small island, whereas there is none in the Rio de Tabasco; that Herrera further speaks of a ford by which the soldiers of Cortes "crossed the river," which would have been impossible in the Tabasco; and finally that the same writer mentions cacao plantations, though at present none exist near Frontera. For these reasons he thinks both Grijalva and Cortes entered the embouchure now known as the Barra de Dos Bocas, some twenty-five miles west of the mouth of the Rio de Tabasco.

A slight examination dissipates these objections. Both Grijalva and Cortes note the powerful current of the Rio de Tabasco, carrying fresh water six miles out to sea, as is observed to-day,[7-1] and this is not in the least applicable to the insignificant stream flowing out of the Dos Bocas. M.

Charnay was misinformed when he stated there is no island at the mouth of the Rio de Tabasco. There are in fact two, one, long and narrow, known as the Isla de Grijalva, the other quite small, close to the plantation of Dolores (see the map). The latter was probably that to which Cortes retired. None of the accounts say that the soldiers "forded the river," but only the short distance between the island and the mainland. These islands give to the entrance of the river the appearance of two embouchures or mouths. The depth of the bar varies of course with the seasons and with the tides.

But what is conclusive is that in 1525 the Spaniards founded the city Nuestra Señora de la Victoria, on the site of Potonchan. In 1646, it had a cura and a vicar, and counted 2000 parishioners, and the abundance of its cacao harvest is especially noted.7-2 At some later day it was attacked and destroyed by filibusters; but the remains of the church and the cemetery are still visible at Dolores, and pilgrimages are yet made to them on certain holy days by the faithful of the parish of Frontera, on the opposite shore. This record places the scene of the conflict beyond all doubt.

Condition of the Natives.—The various accounts agree in describing the province as highly cultivated and thickly settled. Maize and cacao were the principal crops. Temples and edifices are repeatedly referred to. A few years afterwards (1524) Cortes traversed Tabasco some miles inland, and has left a description of its industries. The people were active merchants, and the list of their commodities which he gives includes cacao, maize, cotton, dye-stuffs, feathers, salt, wax, resins, paints, gum copal, pottery, beads, shells, precious stones, woven stuffs and gold of low alloy. The richer citizens had numerous wives and female slaves, which accounted for the rapid increase in population.8-1 The chronicler Gomara furnished a long list of the native articles which Grijalva brought back in 1519 from Potonchan and the neighboring coast. They reveal a high degree of artistic culture, and leave no doubt but that the tribes of the vicinity were as developed in the arts as any in America.

Ruined Cities.—Writing about 1875, Mr. H. H. Bancroft says: "On the immediate coast (of Tabasco) some large towns and temples were seen by the early voyagers; but I have no information that relics of any kind have been discovered in modern times."8-2

In fact, although it is doubtful if there are any ruins directly on the coast, there are many but a short distance inland. Those at Comalcacalco have been figured and described by M. Charnay, and his work is so well known that a reference to it is sufficient.

At the locality called Pedrito, about fifteen miles from the mouth of the Tabasco, there are many mounds, embankments, piles of pottery and other signs of an ancient town. Among the relics is a large circular stone, "like a round table," with figures in relief engraved on its sides, and with holes drilled in its surface, in which pegs or wooden nails are said to have been fitted.8-3 About ten miles north of this spot is another group of mounds on the left bank of the Rio de San Pablo y San Pedro. Doubtless many others exist unknown in the dense forests.

The Ruins of Cintla.—The ruins of Cintla were visited and surveyed by the late Dr. C. H. Berendt in March and April, 1869, and, so far as I know, neither before nor since have they been seen by any archæologist. Nor can I learn that Dr. Berendt ever published the results of his researches. The only reference I can find to them in any of his published writings is in a paper which he read, July 10th, 1876, before the American Geographical Society, and which was published in its Bulletin, No. 2, for that year. The title of this address was, "Remarks on the Centers of Ancient Civilization in Central America and their Geographical Distribution." He certainly prepared a much more extended paper especially on Cintla, with illustrations and maps, fragments of which I have found among the documents left at his death; but if published, I have been unable to trace it. Nor can I discover what became of the considerable archæological collection which he made at Cintla and brought away with him, a memorandum about which is among his papers.

The passage in his address before the Geographical Society touching on Cintla is as follows:

"It was by mere chance that in the year 1869 I discovered the site of ancient Cintla, buried in the thick and fever-haunted forests of the marshy coast, and unknown until then to the Indians themselves. In the course of the excavations which I caused to be made, antiquities of a curious and interesting character were laid bare.

"Prominent among these ruins, and presenting a peculiar feature of workmanship, are the so-called *teocallis*, or mounds, which here are built of earth, and covered at the top and on the sides with a thick layer of mortar in imitation of stone work. On one of these mounds I found not only the sides and the platform, but even two flights of stairs, constructed of the same apparently fragile but yet enduring material. One of the latter was perfectly well preserved. I likewise saw clay figures of animals covered with a similar coating of mortar or plaster, thus imitating sculptured stone and retaining traces of having been painted in various colors.

Fig. 1.—Map of the Ruins of Cintla.

"The reason for this singular use of cement probably is that in the alluvial soil of this coast, no stones occur within a distance of fifty miles and more from the sea shore; stone implements, such as axes, chisels, grinding stones, obsidian flakes, etc., which are occasionally found, can have been introduced solely by trade. The pottery and the idols made of terra cotta show a high degree of perfection.

"Regarding the period down to which such earthenware was made, a broken vase disinterred from one of the mounds in my presence may give a clue. Its two handles represent Spaniards, with their European features, beard, Catalonian cap, and *polainas*, or gaiters."

There is also among his papers the commencement of an address or essay upon these ruins, written in Spanish, and this, when completed, may have been printed in some Mexican periodical. I translate from it the following passage, the remainder having been lost:

"Having learned that in the forests of the coast between the *barras* of Chiltepec and Grijalva various mounds, idols and other remains of an earlier population had been discovered, I proceeded to that part of the country called *Del Cajete*, and devoted six weeks to its exploration. I soon found numerous mounds and embankments from which the present inhabitants had gathered fragments of idols and milling stones of a form unknown now in the vicinity.

"It very soon became apparent that these mounds were not such as those isolated ones which are found in various parts of this country, but were arranged in groups surrounding open spaces, *plazas*, and forming streets, extending over an area three leagues in length by one in breadth.

Fig. 2.—The Great Temple.   **Fig. 3.—Cross Section of Fig. 2, B.**

"Not a single tradition, not a single native name survives to cast any light upon these ruins. The whole of this coast was depopulated in the seventeenth and eighteenth centuries owing to the slave-hunting incursions of the filibusters and man-hunters. The Indians who are now found in the neighborhood have removed there from the interior since the beginning of the present century, and are absolutely ignorant of the origin or builders of this city, hidden in the tropical forest."

The locality referred to as *Del Cajete* was a settlement (rancheria) of Indians, now better known as San José de la Bellota, on a large pond into which drains the Río de la Bellota. It was founded in 1815 by a cura who brought the Indians there from the other side of the river, back of Frontera.

The general position of the ruins will be seen from the above map. It is drawn to the scale of the Mexican league, which contains 5000 yards (varas) each 838 mm. One league is therefore approximately two and three quarters of our miles. No ruins or mounds were located immediately on or near the coast.

Almost a continuous line of mounds, embankments and heaps of débris extends from near Bellota for about nine miles in a general west-south-west direction over a plain which is now densely covered by a tropical forest.

Dr. Berendt did not attempt to survey but a few of these numerous monuments. The plan of one of the largest, called by the natives *El Cuyo Grande*, "The Great Temple," is shown in the following, figure 2.

The principal mound B is terraced about half way up and was 82 feet in height. A cross section of it is shown in Fig. 3, A-B.

A series of constructions is connected with this, the whole running in a direction east-north-east to west-south-west. They consist of a rectangular embankment six to eight feet high, Fig. 2, A; an isolated circular mound, D; and two small mounds at the eastern corners of the great mound, from which parallel embankments, E, extend easterly, inclosing an open space, which at the extremity is terminated by a long low mound, C. The total distance from A to C is 1140 feet.

The great mound and most of the others in the vicinity are faced with mortar made of sand and lime from burnt oyster shells. On one or both sides are flights of steps which lead up to the summit. These are constructed of layers of mortar, tiles and hard-pounded earth, distributed in the manner represented in Fig. 4.

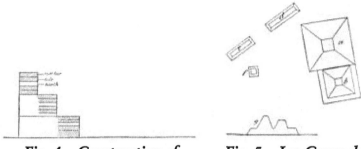

Fig. 4.—Construction of Stairways.

Fig. 5.—Los Cuyos de la Canada.

The earth is either black or red, and is mixed with sand from the coast to give it consistency. The tiles or bricks are rectangular in shape, well made and regular in outline, and laid one against another as in a pavement.

Another group is called *Los Cuyos de la Canada*, Fig. 5. It consists of two mounds on a low platform, adjoining each other. The larger, *a*, is twenty feet in height, the lower, *b*, about fifteen feet. Their sides are oriented exactly to the true north. A section is shown in Fig. 5, *g*. Two small oblong mounds, *c* and *d*, about six feet high, and a square altar-like heap, *f*, appear to be in relation to the group. Numerous pieces of mortar and terra cotta occur in the vicinity, and 1500 feet directly west there is a large mound of moderate height.

Almost anywhere in the area of this ancient city, the soil abounds in fragments of mortar, pottery and images of earthenware. Very frequently the latter are represented seated on a bell-shaped support, apparently that they might be stood up upon a flat surface. Two of these are shown from Dr. Berendt's drawings in Figs. 6 and 7. The handles of utensils were often decorated in fantastic forms as that shown in Fig. 8.

Fig. 6—Image with Bell-shaped Bottom and Handle.

Fig. 7.—Image of a Warrior on Bell-shaped Support.

Fig. 8.— Decorated Handle of Utensil.

An abundance of *metates*, or corn-stones, of a shape not now usual in the neighborhood were exhibited. Some of these were quite graceful, having several feet and highly ornamented. The vases of pottery were occasionally noteworthy for their symmetry and beauty, as that shown in Fig. 9.

Fig. 9.—Jar of Pottery.

At the foot of the stairways to the summit of the mounds on each side were frequently the remains of tigers' heads, well moulded in burnt clay.

Here and there the remains of wells were discovered, or of excavations which apparently were intended for the purpose of obtaining water.

Dr. Berendt mentions several tombs, but unfortunately does not specify their location or construction. He states that they usually contained several bodies, in a sitting posture, placed side by side with their arms and ornaments.

No trace of metal whatever was discovered, neither copper nor gold, which is rather unexpected, as the natives in the time of Grijalva were acquainted with both these substances.

Such is the brief account I am able to give of these extensive and interesting ruins from the fragmentary papers of their explorer. If any reader of these notes can inform this journal of the disposition Dr. Berendt made of his collection and the full memoranda of his surveys and excavations, the cause of American archæology will be further benefited.

3-1 The authorities are:

Carta de la Justicia de la Rica Villa de la Vera Cruz, July 10, 1519. This is sometimes referred to as Cortes' first letter.

Bernal Diaz del Castillo, *Historia de la Conquista de la Nueva Espana.*

Andres de Tapia. *Relacion Sobre la Conquista de la Nueva Espana.*

Relacion Anonyma de la Conquista de la Nueva Espana.

3-2 Francisco Lopez de Gomara, *Conquista de Mexico.* I follow the Madrid edition of 1852.

4-1 This delectable surgical item is added by Captain Bernal Diaz.

5-1 *Historia de las Indias.* Lib. XIV.

5-2 I have consulted both the original edition (1632) and the Madrid reprint of 1852. It is thus spelled in both, though Dr. Jourdanet, in his excellent French translation (Paris, 1877) gives *Cintla.*

6-1 Herrera, *Historia de las Indias Occidentales.* Dec. III, lib. vii, cap. iii.

6-2 Jose N. Rovirosa, *Nombres Geographicos de Tabasco,* (Mexico, 1888).

6-3 Orozco y Berra, *Historia Antigua de Mexico,* Tom. XIV, Lib. I, cap. V.

6-4 I use the French edition, *Les Anciennes Villes du Nouveau Monde,* pp. 159, 160 (Paris, 1885).

7-1 Requena says the current from the river is visible "from ten to twelve leagues from the shore in every season and in high water much further." Pedro Requena, *Informe sobre Tabasco*, p. 52 (S. Juan Bautista, 1847. Imprenta del Gobierno).

7-2 These facts are given in the *Memoria* of Diaz de la Calle, printed at Madrid, 1646, extracts from which I find in Dr. Berendt's manuscripts.

8-1 Cortes' description is given in his "fourth letter." His route is extremely difficult to locate accurately.

8-2 *The Native Races of the Pacific States*, Vol. IV, p. 287.

8-3 MSS, Notes of Dr. C. H. Berendt.